99 Theses to Build Back Better

Authored by:

Adriaan Kamp- Founder Energy For One World

1st December, 2020

"In the beginner's mind there are many possibilities,

but in the expert's there are few."

Shunryu Suzuki (1905-1971)

(1st version, updated version)

Preface

Over the year 2020, and in the Corona virus crisis, our global leadership invented three drivers, three themes and slogans- and that are meant to help our world to a better place:

1. The Great Reset (due to Corona)

2. To Build Back Better

3. The Decade of Action

Now, nationally and internationally, governments, politicians, diplomats, institutes, bankers, economists, industrialists, businessmen and women, academics, scientists, educators, societies are giving their "own words and meanings"- their preferred or recommended lists- of what and where it is- our world needs and do: to build back better.

It will not surprise you- these lists (and action plans) are seldom the same, aligned and attuned- but have much in common in and between each other, and experts and scientists rightly ask themselves: will the change by our Leadership be timely, deep, honest and real enough?.

We have now 5 years experience with the program and deliveries from the Paris Climate Agreement, Energy-Economy Transition/ Reform and the UN SDGs.- and each of you may hold his or her own opinion.

But quite safely I could state: we are yet missing the point, the focus, the directness, the idea, the Plan, the organisation and the momentum to be good for our world.

So, these 99 Theses are from my hand. I created and collated these - over the last decade and most notably this year - and based on this working practice, professional life-time experience and experimental discovery work on Global Change, Energy- Economy Architecture Transition, Paris Climate Agreement, UN SDGs and our Leadership, thereover.

These Theses are here to guide and inspire you- and in our joint wish and effort to Build Back Better- in our Great Reset and our Decade of Action.!

I am sure that governments, politicians, diplomats, institutes, bankers, economists, industrialists, businessmen and women, academics, scientists, educators, societies of good-will can come forward with their own 99 theses, honest and real.

And that is now exactly the point, and what, I Believe- we, our world, now needs and want

We want to deepen our understanding, inspire more open, creative and richer conversations, advance our learning, and organize and enable a true reform- of what today is becoming so clearly broken.

I welcome you to these 99 theses!

Context

We know that we live in one of the better times, ever. If you were to choose in what time and age you wanted to be born- wherever on this planet, this time it is, most likely.

However, we also know that "this Party" is not coming without some concerns.- Geo-political, economic, socially, ecological, technological - and - in and between the rivalries of People, Businesses and Nations.

It was Charles Dickens who gave word to some famous lines in world literature, and with his historic novel "A Tale of Two Cities". It was the time just before and at the great French revolution, and the story tells about the economic, social and political unrest and revolt around these days.

Quote

It was the best of times, it was the worst of times, it was the age of wisdom, it was the age of foolishness, it was the epoch of belief, it was the epoch of incredulity, it was the season of Light, it was the season of Darkness, it was the spring of hope, it was the winter of despair, we had everything before us, we had nothing before us, we were all going direct to Heaven, we were all going direct the other way ...

Unquote

And now we are with Covid- 19: A world "in crisis".

Covid-19 has struck our societies, and we see our life, economies, companies and people in a standstill and/or a lockdown.

Uncertain about their future. Uncertainties about their future household, health, wealth and income.

Early estimate sees worldwide a rise of a new 350 million jobless (at least) , 1.5 billion workers at risk in developing economies, and the global world economy loaded with an unprecedented debt of 277 trillion USD,- and that is 3,65 times what the world earns in a year.

Developed and developing economies are prognosed to shrink over 2020 (-4.4%)- (202x) (except China).

The big brother nations, USA and China have been in a strategic rivalry over the period, with Propaganda and "war of words" being exchanged. Biden Presidency here a possible relief.

The present world is "missing in cohesion and action" over the pandemic, and making SG Guterres gasp in desperation: the world is presently too fragile and not able to come together to face a crisis such as Covid-19: individual countries look after themselves, and not willing to share or care for the common, though the latest breakthroughs on vaccine development- hopeful.

The Oil sector, internationally, is in disarray- as "a power fight" is on-going over the dominion over the markets, and this in combination with the Covid Crisis and demand fall, proofs near lethal for the outlook for the shareholder owned western majors (and related value chains, industries- also: airlines, hospitality, travel, events, cultural, etc.)

Add to this,

The rather poor outlook on the sustainability of (the aggregate of) our economies versus the natural world.

The Corona Virus Crisis placed in our moment in time: From an international perspective: The urgent need for a new narrative: "we are in crisis".

Year 2015 is and has been a Pivot Year in the international community and energy land. First of all, and at the end of 2015- we have seen and experienced the results of years' of climate change negotiations: the Paris Climate Change Agreement. In September of 2015, the UN agreed to embark on a groundbreaking program of capacity and capability building in the realms of Sustainable Development.

Earlier that year, we could listen to the voice of Pope Francis (Encyclical Laudato Si!, Fratelli Tutti)- and learn from Professor Jeffrey Sachs and John Rockstrom that we are accelerating ourselves and crossing some planetary boundaries- and also ourselves. We were "in crisis"

In all of these programs- Energy and the direction of our Economies are crucial and vital elements for our common home and our success.

Stewardship over the Energy Sector and Economy Direction/ Architecture developments and UN Sustainable Developments allowing and enabling the rise of sustainable societies, individually- and in aggregate- is a new leadership role to learn- in, between and for governments and the business community.

In some very simple terms- one could state that we – and over the coming 10-20 years has the following goals to attain, and in order to stave off some serious :

-Recover from the Corona virus crisis
- Support the UN Sustainable development goals
- Help implement the Paris Climate Change Agreement
- Sustain Energy to our Societies- for sustainable economies.

In essence:

How to provide energy and build sustainable (consumption) economies – whilst recognizing that we are to share one planet- in harmony in and between themselves- and with energy-economies that are sustainable, affordable and available- free of concerns- and for generations to come.

And let us be honest, before the Corona Virus Crisis- both Chairman Xi JinPeng, President Trump, PM Modi, President Putin, Saudi Leadership and most leadership in Europe stood on the gas pedal of their economies, competing and rivaling to gain Country GDP and jobs, and where nowhere near into the direction of Paris Climate Change agreement, or the achievement of the UN SDGs.

Global Change (General)

1. Earlier, World Scientists have spoken, and have warned our world that we have about 10 years left "to get our acts together". In essence, and over the last decades- it has ever become so clear that our present forms of economies has become a caricature- of its original intents, at best.:

    a. The "Cost" to Planet Earth and Our Nature, the "Cost of Over-using our Earth Resources (from Next Generations)"- has now, and over the last decades- so ample been described by Scientists, Activists, and Leadership, at large.
    From the loss of biodiversity, species, fauna and flora, jungles, mis-use of land for intense farming, towards over-fishery of our seas, polluting our world with plastics, pesticides and chemistry- towards the great risks we have created ourselves in with burning fossil

fuels, abundantly and unconstrained, into our lungs and atmospheres, and with few eyes on quality of earth reserves in the ground. Climate Change not the least.
75% of natural land has been touched by the intense economies of the human hand, and only 2% of the seas is yet left without a boat.
b. Both WWF (2020) and IPBES (2019) reports a rapid deterioration and loss of our biodiversity, with a 6th mass extinction – bigger, worse and more alarming as ever believed before.
c. We may have long passed the 1.5 degr threshold target, and the way the oil and gas industry is and was ticking before Covid- we were running ourselves towards a 3-5 degrees C warming by century end. re. Hansen- Nasa (2013), Randers-Club of Rome (2020), Rockstrom (2020), Concerned Scientists (2018-2019).
d. The IPCC reports that the impacts of a 1.5 Degrees world is worse then expected. Our present best

estimate, and with current trends and rate of fossil fuels consumption, is that our world is galloping towards a 3.6 Degrees Celsius world, over this century (and even higher if we not manage to bend the present trend in the oil and gas sector)

e. The UNEP report in its latest Emission Gap Report 2018 is that the gap between that the world needs to up three-fold its present effort in cleaning-up its act, if we are to have any chance at all to stay within the 2 Degrees.

f. Our Oceans are heating-up, our corals are disappearing, we are over-fishing, and the plastic soup is ever so great , and barely stoppable as emerging and rapid developing nations install new petrochemical complexes.

g. Our food chains are unsustainable and broken, we have introduced unsustainable ways of intense farming and agriculture, and we see and prognose fresh water shortages, and our global health organisations and medics warn us

for the air we breath in our dense cities and industries.
h. Our soils are eroding, and our natural forests are depleting at an alarming rate-
i. We are already crossing some 24 planetary boundaries, and the rapidization of our (global) societies and liberal free markets- are still destroying social fabric on the go, and in the views of Germany Kathrin Hartmann: we are presently living in "the Green Lie"
j. Both the UN, Human Rights Watch and Amnesty International report that the Human Rights in our world seemingly- "looks and feels"- not to have progressed over the last decade(s). Instead they report ever more countries, with ever more governments, taking it not so narrow with the (individual) human rights, the amount of human right violations on the rise, and that the international dialogues on these issues stalled, politicized, and the works of the human rights organisations have become more

difficult, forbidden- and in the worst case killed.
k. In 2018, Angela Merkel observed: there are 220 armed conflicts on our Planet, with 65 million refugees, with half of them children.
l. Prof Sachs reminds us "A market system produces wealth but it does not produce social justice . . . The the desire for wealth. It has to be tempered by the demands of morality, ethics."
m. In the more sobering words of the French SocioGraph Christophe Guilluy: we are presently creating "No Societies", and the world income equality all to rise: Go to World Inequality Report
n. or in the words of Pope Francis : the wealthy few feast on what belongs to all

2. The club of Rome held its 50th anniversary– and well – concluded, we are running exactly on their curves of 1968.:

> *In the words of Weiszacker:*
> *We are in (desperate) need of a new form of Enlightenment, and where Balance would become a new notion between Humans and Nature, Short-term and Long-term, Public and Private, Religion and State, Feminine and Masculine, Equity and Rewards, Speed and Stability.*

3. Begin November 2020, Johan Rockstrom- Professor at the Resilience Center at Stockholm- shared his latest call for our urgency and action (and I strongly ask you to watch, in full):
"10 years to transform the future of humanity -- or destabilize the planet"

4. Our political theaters, nationally and internationally- seem ever more polarized, with more and more extreme views, lack of cohesion, willingness to collaborate on issues in a multi-lateral and ever so much wanting "to win"- Archim Steiner of the UNDP sees that the international willingness to collaborate on the UN SDGs is stalling at best, backtracking most likely, and that we are hardly re-engineering our approaches in our trade and trade relations.

5. Our present (geo-political, strategic) rivalries in and between the Nations - on and over economies, jobs, market(s) and business dominions, access to resources and nature- prevents us from stepping our world into a better place. Competition and Rivalries, nationally and internationally, prevents us to truly build back better

6. Our Worldview and the way we think, talk and act on our Self, Country, The Other, Economy, Society and Nature matters, and has influence over our governance, market constellations and transition.

7. It was 75 years ago- that Europe was freed from war. And it was 75 years ago, that people, countries, governments and corporations started to recover from the deep wounds of conflict, of war, of poverty, of atrocities, human rights abuses, of fear- and to convert themselves to Hope, Peace and Justice.

    Hope of (re-)building and (re-) constructing their societies
    Hope of building bridges of Peace and Justice: never again (a great) war.
    Hope of building a better world for their children and grandchildren
    Hope of building a better and socially more inclusive and just economies, here and there

    New institutes and organisations were imagined, instigated and created- from the United Nations, Human Rights, towards new Universities and Academies to learn new leadership and diplomacy for a better world.

It was a period of Great Hope, Can-do and (Re-)Imagination. Can we re-do this again at our Great reset?

How do we envision the world to be - over the coming 75 years?

8. To my mind, the present uncertainties and urgent change challenge in our geo-politics, societies, economies, energy architectures, recovery and in order to attain planetary sustainability asks experience in and with (large scale multidimensional change program) execution and realization, and asks us also to be little bit more integral and holistic, a little bit more humble and servant, but also to be much more discerning, pragmatic, open, situational, responsible and direct where and how we attain true change in our societies , our businesses and trades, and in this more complex constellation- than some lengthy words and global commissions with glossy reports (promoting solutions).

9. Lets focus on one or two..
    a. To agree and know where we are in control, things are going great, and we can let the market free and does it work.
    b. To agree and know where things are not so great, and urgent action and attention is needed
    c. To agree and know what and where to change, and direct governments and corporations to change direction and governance ways, the trades and the market (rules).
    d. And to agree what we do not yet know, where there is uncertainty, or where we are way out of control.

10. The eyes of Sir David Attenborough and the Eyes of the Holy See, Pope Francis- : their message(s) were clear: about our Planetary Boundaries, about our Human

Developement, and about our social inter-relations and context.

Progress in our Human Development is achieved, if each (re. our) generation manages to pass-over a World which is "better", more hopeful, peaceful and "lighter" towards the (coming, next) generation, following.

In 2010, it was Dominique Mosie, who shared "his views and eyes" onto the apparent era of [the Geopolitics of Emotions](), we were seeing and getting ourselves in.

The era, where Asia would see and note "a New Sunrise of Hope", and *of every day a bit better day*, and whereby the ruling (past) of the West would live by the notion of some Despair: every day a bit less and more uncertainties about its future.

Well, in short, the Covid pandemic has given us that world- today.

Whilst the West is presently occupied with their decade of "the decay of truth" (or "Decade of Decay" -in some viewers eyes) (re. Also Tweet- Obama) - between the political factions and society in the US, and between the countries in Europe (e.g. Brexit, Trust, etc.),

China- and with its ambition to become World Leader- has set a new tone and standard (and in its decoupling strategy from USA):

in Hanoi, and in November 2020, 15 Asian Countries with a population of over 2.2 billion people signed the RCEP

A true (new) Magnet for future national, business, military, and natural resource securities: "The Century of Asia".

The Century that Asia is going to determine who or what *is* in this world.

11. In 2018, a former friend of my (we befriended in Syria Damascus, already

back in the early, mid-90s) became the Dutch Permanent Representative to the UN Security Council.

Most recently, and in April 2020- he has published a book on this year, his experiences and learning insights:

From the Book: **Met een Oranje Jas**

> *In his book "With an orange tie", Ambassador Karel van Oosterom gives the reader an intimate insight into the Security Council, where he held a coveted post for the Netherlands in 2018. He describes how diplomats fought international conflicts without flying at each other's throats, and how the The Council helped prevent Ebola from becoming a global pandemic, even though tensions in Syria, Yemen, Iran and North Korea,...were already underway that year. of the UN and what it means to the Netherlands that it was a member of the Security Council for a year. (Note Text: Google Translate from Dutch)*

Now - Karel and I have communicated a little on the contents of his book, but also on the present, and the true urgencies and importances for reform.

In his words : the world and the security council has not become better, then it was in 2018. And he is concerned

My formal, agreed and published comment to his Book:

Van Oosterom has written a Page Turner, and in a very beautiful and special way expresses his experiences as elected in the Security Council and determined them for future generations.

What a year, and what an experience and clever how van Oosterom has given here - on behalf of all of us - improvements and improvements in Peace and Security, and the functioning of the Security Council.

...

> *Van Oosterom's closing words about the future are less in Diplomatic terms, and the desired (or urgent and introduced) changes to the Council, its organization, and the reality of today spur and encourage all of us to consider and make it possible (in our work and diplomacy) from transcending our National or Self-Interest to organizing a sustainable foundation for a more General Interest of Peace and Security "- in our" Common Home ".*
>
> (Note Text: Google Translate from Dutch)

12. Every Country and Every Organisation in this World can be improved upon in order to raise the human, social, economic and sustainable development to all.

Paris Climate Agreement

13. The present approach towards Climate Change is One-dimensional- and the approach to steer Energy Architecture

Change (developments) on Carbon Price, ETS and CCS (in the West) may proof illusory and bound to fail, as are the- at times- very complex mechanisms in the Paris Agreement hard to see to effectively come to work. (measuring, reporting, verifying: Climate Finance, Compliance, Transparancy, Loss and Damage, National Reporting, Technology transfer and mechanism, etc.)

    a. Our Oil Company executives knew this , and as they lobbied for this to be.
  For as it stands:

    b. Are you to ask the Turkey to prepare for the Christmas meal?

14. CO_2 pricing, etc is a derivative and *indirect* working method- does not solve the root-cause, and is an accountancy and transparency nightmare (or consultancy heaven!), and is not likely to work well under changing energy market pricings, popular vote or industry lobby.

    It's a solution of the "Rich men world".

It is far better to work directly and on direct improvements of our energy architecture solutions, and to make "Energy Free of Concerns"- here and there - now and tomorrow.

An example of how you may then speak, think and act- can be found in this conversation: Go to Conversation.: How to decarbonize the Grid and Electrify everything.

15. People, "experts and institutes" , Corporates and Nations, and who occupy themselves and solely pledge and lobby (in between themselves) to fight and combat Climate Change, to see to put a goal, policies, price and target on CO_2 emissions, put it in the ground, invent derivatives, complex programs (e.g. G20 4 Cs) , and who encourage, promote and believe in technical solutions and innovations (or substitutes e.g. Hydrogen, Biofuels, etc.) to limit CO_2 in our rise of Nations, , - act largely *one-dimensional*, also in their self-interests, and in the

proposed and envisioned energy-economy architecture changes and transition,

16. and - to my mind and practice view- "*do not get it*", - in what true global *system* change challenge we see ourselves today, and what opportunities and discoveries for Change, and to develop ourselves, we have to make.: They miss *the key point.*

17. Michael Mooreś bombshell documentary "Planet of the Humans"- on some of the hidden truths in the so-called Green Transition and Green growth agenda in the USA:.

Three concerns, and according to this documentary:

a. Some "Green Evangelicals" have gone to bed with "Mainstream Businesses, "lobbied and promoted", and to see personally or organisational benefits from these accords: Green Greed.

b. The idea that we simply can and have to replace fossil fuels with Wind, Solar, Bio, Electric Cars - and can continue our life as we know it - is simply untrue. Plus:

CO2 is not the only problem in the environment (re. e.g. the destruction of jungle forest at the closing of the movie): it's multi-dimensional. In addition, there are some serious concerns with mining for rare earth, supply chains and siting/ use of these new technologies.

c. If we do not change the above narrative, our lifestyle and our approach in our reform (less is more), we waste time and will miss the point of sustainability, and help our humanity unnecessary into the abyss.

As I am personally not a fan of the style and ways of this sort of documentary, I must admit that the three key messages in his documentary- i can relate to, and that I can see great merit and courage in his efforts to disclose, and to get ourselves into some better form of more richer and open conversations and program of works.

That i fully agree.

Less is Mo(o)re.

The approach and ways we elected "to work" the Paris Agreement, and given the above, was clearly non functional- and is urgently in need of a better form.

18. (as an example of a week) Over the week of 15th June, I attended (and enjoyed) a global webinar conference celebrating 20 years UN Global Compact, but where I also heard consultants encouraging the business community for "speed and technology" to accelerate and to "recover better" and some rather empty words from dignitaries and leadership around ,

    I attended the (launch of the) 69th edition of the World Energy Statistics by BP, a presentation by the Economist Intelligence Unit on the Economic Outlook- post-Covid-19, a book launch by Professor Sachs, a launch of taxonomy by Frans Timmermans of the EU, and a new product launch from the IEA- with a steep warning for climate change, and over the next years..

    Different lenses - on our (seemingly) ever more complex and demanding world of today and tomorrow.

I planned to share you here some brief summaries and my observations of these events, and words spoken, but after attending "all this circus of well-meant but also glossy words from our Globalites, some good-to-great panels and leadership examples (!), some sense and quite some nonsense- I crossed the words spoken by a teenager on the Swedish Radio.

And she hitted the nail right on the head- of what I also observed (over last decade) , and can easily state and share this,with you- as well.

Our present Globalites (on average and in majority) "don't get it", are surely part of the problem in their fads- in their trained habits , eagerness and greed of self-importance and self -promotion, their form of approach and organisation, won't bring us the leadership behaviors, or the more healthier, honest, simpler, direct and more natural solutions - that we need to nurture, foster, seek and need.

Now, the teenager I refer to, here is Greta Thunberg- and she is here quite focused on one-dimension: Climate Change.

19. In Greta Thunberg (own) words:

She describes world leaders queuing to get pictures with her, with Angela Merkel asking whether it was okay to post her photo on social media

The climate campaigner is sceptical of their motives. "Perhaps it makes them forget the shame of their generation letting all future generations down", she says. "I guess maybe it helps them to sleep at night."

"All that is left are empty words", she says.

The phrase reflects her deep cynicism about the motives of most world leaders.

"The level of knowledge and understanding even among people in power is very, very low, much

lower than you would think," she told the BBC.

She says the only way to reduce emissions on the scale that is necessary is to make fundamental changes to our lifestyles, starting in developed countries. But she doesn't believe any leaders have the nerve to do that.

Instead, she says, they "simply refrain from reporting the emissions, or move them somewhere else".

She claims the UK, Sweden and other countries do this by failing to account for the emissions from ships and aircraft and by choosing not to count the emissions from goods produced in factories abroad.

As a result, she says in her radio programme, the whole language of debate has been degraded.

"Words like green, sustainable, 'net-zero', 'environmentally friendly', 'organic', 'climate-neutral' and 'fossil-free' are today so misused and watered down that they have pretty much lost all their meaning. They can imply everything from deforestation to aviation, meat and car industries," she said.

Ms Thunberg says the only positive that could come out of the coronavirus pandemic would be if it changes how we deal with global crises: "It shows that in a crisis, you act, and you act with necessary force."

She says she is encouraged that politicians are now stressing the importance of listening to scientists and experts.

"Suddenly people in power are saying they will do whatever it takes since you cannot put a price on human life."

She hopes that will open up a discussion about the urgency of taking action to help the people who die from illnesses related to climate change and environmental degradation right now as well as in the future.

But she remains deeply pessimistic about our ability to keep any temperature increases within safe boundaries.

She says that, even if countries actually deliver the carbon reductions they've promised, we'll still be heading for a "catastrophic" global temperature rise of 3-4 degrees.

20. (and in correspondence with a senior executive on strategy/ scenario making in one of our Leading Multinational Oil & Gas companies) : Don't you think that our world is changing now in unexpected ways, and that your planned and controlled phasing towards 2050 seems a little out of touch and outdated, and that our world is desperately seeking and needing a little more creative and urgent ways in reforming our economies, our consumption patterns and the ways we transform our energy architectures- in order to attain sustainable, durable and socially just societies? If one thing is sure, our Corona pandemic has shown that status quo and so-called fixed or market rules are all up for scratch, and worth not so much more (in value and values).

The other reality is that our beloved industry also opted to choose and lobby for a Paris Agreement that was focused on derivatives, not on true or meaningful change. Paris was never to go to meet the

Climate Change needs or ambitions. In addition, and that is the real omission, we forgot to see and include the other realities into considerations: Geopolitics of Emotions and the Planetary Boundaries we are in. Our invitation now is to correct this, and come forwards with plans and proposals that can help and work. Everything else is just entertainment."

21. Ever since Obama walked into the hallways of COP15 in Copenhagen, we, the world knew, that Climate Change and the later deal made in Paris can become a Pandora's box of unknowns, and new unpleasantries- in and between the rise of Nations. The ways by which the BRICS and China + 77 nations have argued and defended the "common but differentiated responsibilities"- at home, in the media, and at the international conferences and accords- tells here a lot.

    Think about the situation where every storm, every flood, every drought in Bangladesh and beyond is named to be the result of Western Lifestyle and historic cultural insensitivities, greed and egoism.

Think again about the mother or father who sees his children and family lost (in such a situation).

Think again if the survivors wish to leave and flee their Land and Home(s), and see themselves stranded at the (western) gates, walls or seas to a safe haven.

And Think again, if you combine this with some new and freshened historical awareness of the colonial times and past, of the West- in the East and in the South.

True of False, Yes, we the People, The Leaders in our (energy-economy) community better get real, and see ourselves to work, to change, and to create true bridges of Peace, Can-Do and Good.

22. To Push "harder" at something that did not work before, does not make it better or necessary to work. Change (in working approach, ambition, goals) may be needed, when goals and plans are clearly out of reach.

UN Sustainable Development Goals

23. It is in our Energy Trade and Trade relations that we can make our biggest gains on Energy, Climate and UN SDGs. Peace, Energy and UN SDGs are here deeply intertwined.

24. The UN GLobal Compact asks, invites, begs us to realize a new formula between Energy, Climate and UN SDGs- in exploitation and developing nations:

    a. Roadmap 2030= COVID Recovery + (Oil & Gas Developments) + New Energy Architecture + Finance + Good Stewardship + Jobs in the Non-energy Economy + Economy Reform+ Paris Agreement + UN SDGs 2030.

25. The path of building back better and transition towards Sustainable Societies asks us to realize several transitions in parallel:
    a. Strengthening human well-being and capabilities

b. Shifting towards sustainable and just economies that support and serve human well-being and balance with nature
   c. Building sustainable food systems and healtly nutrition patterns
   d. Achieving energy decarbonization and universal access to energy
   e. Promoting sustainable urban, rural and peri-urban lifestyles and development
   f. Securing the global environmental commons

26. Large Corporations have taken-up the habit to publish ('integrated, holistic") <u>Company Sustainability Report over the years.</u> If it were to my hands, this Form of Sustainability Reporting- on own company operations, own (!) projects, and handling- can to my mind go to the library or shelves, as it serves no wider purpose or meaning, than to show "how good i am".

Hopeful purpose and meaning is derived when we know-how to use and reform our Company Capabilities, our Company Role,

Function, Story and messages - and give it the new and relevant meaning in the realization of sustainable economies and societies, in full.

That is what the Global Compact is about, and that is what the cry from SG Guterres is all about.

And that may give you a whole different focus, write-up or picture Not on the self, but on the markets, the nations, the functioning of the sector and the whole.

27. The UN released a hand-some report, and on the questions we may pose, and the effects the COVID-19 pandemic has, on the execution and delivery of the 17 Sustainable Development Goals - around the globe.

    Other good questions to ask, are for sure:

    - What are we to learn?

    - Where and how can we do better, as we did before?

    - What (shared) future are we building?

- Are we learning, in our nation and international relationships?

- How can we better organize ourselves, and improve our tone of voice- and in order to better bridge our divides and see ourselves to beget sustainable societies?

Energy and Energy Transition

28. The energy architecture on location is a reflection of the socio-political, economic, ecological and business philosophies, leadership and interests exercised on location.

29. I have come to believe that our time asks us to look differently at Energy ("essential service for human life, human civilization- not just "a commodity" to be traded or profited from, and an industry in need of a new business model) , and , hence, and especially for "the too big to

fail"corporations is not solely to be in the hands of a management supervisory board and shareholders investors. Truly independent civic and sustainable development interests are to be at the table.

30. Without too many words- I suggest you either read the first book of this working practice : Energy For One World,some articles published by my hand or some latest News from my Practice
    a. or read a brief opinion on the present believes "on the abundance of oil and gas" recently published by a <u>senior Shell colleagues (of me) concludes that the world has run out of "easy oil and easy gas"</u>, and that we need to think differently about energy, wealth and wealth creation.:
    b. When we speak about the (reserve) abundance of gas for decades to come, the industry speaks about **unconventional resources of gas**. The present best estimate of conventional gas reserve ("easy to extract") is only 60 years. When we double our gas consumption, these

"easy to get" gas reserves are quickly evaporating. Not a good thing for future generations.

31. Energy Transition is change. Our Present Market System and our Corporate/ Market Governance is to change

32. We have **over-complicated** and **over-bureaucratized** our present working approaches towards Energy, Climate and UN SDGs, and in many governments, ministries and corporates the lack of leadership awareness, competencies and capabilities is at times stunning- both at the OECD, as with the rest.

33. It is relatively easy to provide Energy (comfort, mobility, work) to the Rich, it is a bit more challenging to provide energy to the the Poor. Between Countries and in Countries. Now and tomorrow.

34. We are invited to re-invent the present Power and Energy markets and sectors: nationally, regionally, and internationally. Whilst in the 20st century Oil and Gas were the number One and preferred

sources of supply, the 21st century is served if we know-how to redesign our present homes, cities, cars, transportation and working life- and power these functions from 100% renewables.- and let Oil and Gas become the Last Man, "the Keeper"- in the (energy) value chains. Our focus in the Energy Sector is to be on the engineering, manufacturing and installation capacities, capabilities and volumes we are to realize in and with new energy architectures and product/lifestyle re-designs.

35. The roles and responsibilities of the present incumbents (Large and Major Oil and Gas Corporations IOC/ NOC) in our World Energy System can be greatly advanced:
    a. Today, in and in general, they hold focus on their ways in finding and proving new reserves and to maintain operating envelope and production performances.
    b. However, great advancement can be made if
        i. They would know-better how to be a Leader in the Sector - on Economic Rentability over

       time, Reserves and Sustainability- over time (7 generations), and the outlook of the whole and in the aggregate of the sector.
   ii. Better act as a steward over the developments and transition in the whole energy architecture, change and value chains.
   iii. Integrate UN Sustainable Development in the Business Model of Resource Exploitation
   iv. Actively support the transition from fossil fuel consumption in our cars, homes and service sectors.

36. A good (Oil & Gas) company today is a company that (first and foremost) lobbies, promotes, works and realizes , tirelessly, to replace fossil fuels and get the better energy architectures for our homes, work, cars and modern transportation in place, and strives to leave the reserves, when found, as long as possible in the ground, for future generations.

37. The present multinational energy company (Oil & Gas) boardroom, as it presently is, can -and will to my mind-not easily meet the social responsible roles and sustainable development responsibilities on Energy and Petro-chemistry- these holders actually may seek or have:

38. Two reasons:

    a. I have come to believe that our time asks us to look differently at Energy ("essential service for human life, human civilization- not just "a commodity" to be traded, speculated or profited from, and an industry in need of a new business model) , and , hence, and especially for "the too big to fail"corporations is not solely to be in the hands of a management supervisory board and shareholders investors. Truly independent social, economic and sustainable development interests are to be at the table.

b. The organisational form of the shareholder Company not fit for what our society seeks or need: you cannot serve two masters: either be a (project-)portfolio optimization company, or you are a company serving the national interests on energy architecture and chemical developments- in a region.

39. Global World Energy (Transition) Outlook and Needs differs widely from institutes and corporations: The incumbent OIl and Gas Sector maintains a strong outlook for their Sector, and prognosed a world fuelled by Oil & Gas for decades to come. Both Opec, IEA as well the key and large Oil & Gas corporations in this world see the present fraction of fossil fuels in the total of world energy mix not (significantly) to change till 2040 (80:20). IRENA, the IPCCC and Climate Scientists hold a different lens: for them it is important and without a reasonable doubt, that by 2040, fossil fuels are and have to

be reduced to less than 20% of the global energy mix.

40. A small hidden truth, here, is - that if we were to review **the quality and geographical spread of our world energy reserves**, and especially on oil and gas, we would be shocked:
    a. BP reports all of the found and proven oil and gas reserves, but does not discern between the conventional and unconventional reserves- or hard-to-get, dirty, ecological sensitive and/or highly costly forms of reserves, that our societies rather keeps in the ground (as they are energy-intense, ecological sensitive and/or chemistry-intense).
    b. 10 years ago, the world energy outlook was that we have about 30 years left of conventional, easy-to-produce oil and gas- for the **whole** world.

c. In terms of the essentials for our human civilisation- and in energy land- this means : Tomorrow, or otherwise phrased:
d. This is nothing. Nothing of any serious reserves, and surely not for the next 7 generations.
e. With the arrival of the unconventionals, the dirty shales and fracking in the USA, the reserve numbers have been "pimped-up", but so have the intensity and the unhealthiness of the oil and gas sector in its outlook - for us, and for our planetary boundaries.

41. Our Global (World) Energy System and Outlook would greatly benefit if we, were to:
    a. Have a common system in place, covering energy demand and supply - from the East and the West, the North and the South. (Opec, IEF, IRENA, IEA, UN Energy)

b. To agree on volumes, reserves and distribution of energy commodities and renewables manufacturing & installation capacities, and to prevent the rivalries and competitions over Price, Shortages, Resources, Value Chains, etc.
c. To agree on equitable and durable price settings for least developed nations and developed. Perhaps different prices for different consumers (Rich vs Poor).
d. To agree on sustainable development criteria and programs of the least developed nations, and by our exploitation of their natural resources and endowments.
e. To agree on a (paid) method of World Reserve Keeping- sustainability of fossil fuels - for generations to come.
f. To establish the world capacities and production rates - for oil, gas, renewables.
g. To agree on the rate of transition in the various power blocks (Paris Agreement)
h. To stay positively and constructively engaged and in dialogue and to

work towards a new and better energy architecture for the 21st century, based on goodwill, creation and hope.

42. The Western (OECD-) countries do well if they are able to "make room: and reduce their average fossil energy footprint (including petro-chemicals, plastics) significantly, in order to allow and facility the non-OECD countries to grow and allow their benefits and wealth creation (opportunity) from fossil energy .

43. The general predicted increase in world average energy consumption per capita should ideally be generated by non-fossil fuels such as renewables and re-designs. Overall world fossil fuel production is not to rise and should taper-down significantly if we do not wish to cross (production-volumes) levels which can no longer be sustained or guaranteed for our economies, societies and nature (Climate Change)

44. We need better oversight and agreement on the rules of the game on sustainability and the rather dynamic developments in

the world energy system". We need true policies, markets and regulations which supports the new.

45. We need a business and large (energy) corporation agenda: "making room for the new" enabling the development of energy architectures of the 21 century.

46. Our present *system and leadership* (believes) change challenge is not solely to replace fossil fuels with renewables-, - in a level playing field- unfortunately- but is *much* larger, deeper and wider than that. - and in order to heal and help ourselves and our next generations truly with a chance to see sustainable economies, sustainable societies and sustainable development: And it is in our Worldview, the way we are, relate and see this World (of ours), the Story, that we can make the biggest gain in "our Leadership over the Change".

47. It was OPEC that released in October 2020 its "Flagship World Oil Outlook 2045", and made it rather clear statement that the

time of peak oil was still far out, and that the world of Africa, Asia, Middle-East, Latin-America (South-South) were expected on a development path - unaware of any planetary boundaries, of sorts.

And if you had any doubts on "in what energy landscape world we presently are" - I invite you to listen to the words of Alexander Novak, Energy Minister of Russia, and who in a most recent interview at WEC (World Energy Council) very well phrased the new energy realities he sees us today in.

In a little bit cynical, if not under-cooled statement, he explained that Europe (and the West) have become Resource Craving Regions- and have hence become dependent on foreign import or (new) renewables: In his views, the whole of the Climate Agenda is a bit "over-hyped", and made possible because the West (Europe) has used all of its own natural reserves.

(but he does not dismiss, but agrees and stands-by the Paris Agreement).

48. (and in correspondence on a shareholder meeting of a large Multinational Oil & Gas Company):
Personally, I was a little puzzled why and how much time was spent in this Q&A by shareholders and supervisory board on discussing goals and targets for year 2050.- and actually all in some very wobbly and vague wordings, commitments and acts.

That is 30 years away, from now, and - in a time- when we can hardly look more than a month or two ahead in our time. And who knows what is urgent and important, and on top of our agenda- in energy land- in 10 years from now?

What is the meaning to ask the present CEO to give his exact views on that (year 2050), but fail to ask him what he is to think, direct or act, today?

In addition, and not to make the year 2050-climate targets unimportant, but I failed to see or read any observations on comments by leadership and the shareholders on the thoughts, implications and impact the present oil market fight might have on the strategy, workings and future markets of the companies. And how and when the Company knew this coming, their intelligence, you see...

The one question raised, and in relation with the quality of the reserves of the Company, and the oil price it needs in order to sustain, reform or grow itself- was also quite poorly addressed : in fact- left unanswered.

Not a question was asked what and how was leading or managing the plastic pollution trouble, of our oceans and nature.

The most important question(s) on what roles and responsibilities the Company will assume, now and tomorrow, in the mature and developed (Western, G7) economies and markets on energy transition and energy architecture change and in order to help attain Sustainable Societies (Paris, UN SDGs) , and in their trade and trade relations with developing and emerging markets- was not asked, nor answered.

Neither the question what mix and balance of investment criteria are here of importance (social, economic, sustainability- investment returns vs. social responsibilities), nor how it plans to play a role as interlocutor or as lobbyist in the national and regional plans on energy transition in the various trades: power-markets, fuel sales, transport, industry, etc.

So- in essence, the quality of our debates, dialogues and conversations (in the Boardroom, by shareholders) and with grand organisations on the Purpose, Mission and Plans of a Corporation deserves attention, reform- and some better expertise and gifts.

49. And in an (open) correspondence with Sir mark Moody Stuart on his, otherwise

excellent, message and view on the turmoil in the OIl and Gas Sector:

Perhaps it is not such a good idea for the coming and next generations, that the dominant players in the oil market are now going to pump-up low-cost oil, in fast and furry, and hence affect the quality of reserves for later years.: kicking the bucket of trouble to later.

A system of (quality) reserves maintenance would be a blessing to have- in and between our brotherhood of nations.

Another thing surely to note, and implicitly stated by Sir Mark: the fallout of producers in the West, may cause a new ripple re. defaults with debts and in the financial system - so we may see ourselves here- from crisis to crisis.

Finally, I happen to differ from the roles and responsibilities, and the solutions, incumbent oil and gas majors are invited now to see and do.

50. Understanding "the Energy Game we are in"- can make all the difference.

Leadership, Corporate Governance and Organisation

51. Form Follows Function. There are many ways and many options how we may change the constitution and constellation of Corporate Governance of our present "Too Big To Fail Corporations" in order to achieve an improved and sustainable development outcome

52. The system and corporates that are "too big to fail" may become "too big to safe". So- it is important to Get Real, Get Honest and Get on with it! (statement by Hans vd Loo)

53. Corporate Governance of our Dominant Actors have "an extra duty of care"- in failing states and in the sector. So far-

and what we have seen amd witnessed following the Paris Agreement, Leadership, States (if not a few) and the Sector are and have been failing.

54. We may first have to "heal" our Corporations, before they are ready to be of use and value in the Energy Transition and UN SDGs.

55. Our tone of voice, our style of leadership matters. The invitation we have today is to see and blend our consciousness and care for Deep Humanity and Deep Ecology with our more mainstream energy economies, power and politics- at play.

56. Our ecological crisis is also a psychological or human crisis: in our trust and in our real availability, relationships and presence between each other.

57. On the moment we recognize that "its no longer about the self or our self-importance", but it is much more to do with serving the other and the whole, we may start to become a little less important and create with more Peace.

a. It is "our style", the "way we look" and "our tone of voice" that can move mountains.

b. Not fast, but actually slowing down- and walking in more beauty.

58. The sweet spot of Leadership Transformation is when Leaders balance and instate a healthy and harmonious role and function of Self with the Corporate Organisation, and in relation with Society, the Other, the Whole and Nature- and for over 7 generations.

59. The complex, high-dynamic, rapid change, uncertain 21st century is inviting us to dare to journey into the Nature of Legitimate Power and Greatness: Truly great leaders want to serve the people they lead. They do this by supporting them rather than dictating to them, and by assigning top priority to employee well-being. Deceptively simple, deeply profound, seldomly well done!

60. I believe in the permanence of Value and Values and the Ethics in our Leadership:

Over the last decade, my belief (and based on my international corporate life experience, but also science, facts, insights, experimental work, practice, etc.) is that our best bet for the future of our Common Home today is, is that we see our Global Change challenge as a multi-dimensional invitation to walk in more Peace, in better Relationships, and in more Balance.

61. What is worse: A Leader that speaks-out against Reform, but at least is clear in his goals and intentions, or a Leader who speaks to the ears of his constituencies, but hides his true will or can-do?

    What is worse: over-promise or under-delivery?

    The painful truth is : it has been 7 generations of Leadership (ever since the first Club of Rome report, or 50 years) - in the Large Oil and Gas Corporations, and at the Ministries of Energy and Economy- that have failed to give us our very best, and thus our chance.

It was "The(ir) Crown" - that took them (great, greater, greatest- fast, faster, fastest) so busy.

62. Leadership in Nations, Political parties and Large Corporations have understood that they are in a form of cat - and -mouse game with their constituencies, stakeholders, communities, activists and - at times, also- the scientific community. "The trick" of naming and acknowledging the global change challenge we are in, to design programs and slogans that speak to mainstream public mind ("Build Back Better", "The Great Reset") , and to design (smart) corporate and national programs that gives the illusion of Purpose, Meaning, Change and Inclusiveness- without, at times, truly touching or changing anything relevant in power, organisation, hierarchy, money, interest, or play ("the heart of the matter") - is to sprinkle sand in the eyes of the People, at best- un-ethical and corruption of moral leadership- in more serious cases.

63. In the early phase of my career, and in a certain country (let me be a little generic here), we had a Country Chairman, and his name was Heinz.
Heinz was a characterful man, a true gentleman and leader, and a man of quality and principle.- but Heinz had also one shortfall: in his speeches and interventions- he always looked back, and he would teach us (the younger staff members) - that with "Hind Sight"- we could have done it different, and better.

    You may guess with me-what happened: In no time- we invented a nickname for the poor man: "With Heinz Sight"-and all our mistakes of shortcomings from that day onwards, we made good, with the comment and statement:

    "With Heinz Sight- I would have done this better".

64. And in all this- I came to see,
    a. There are good people in a wrong system, and there are bad people in a good system.

    b. Name me a Country, or a People, who have done no wrong or ill over history- to others?
    c. Name me a Country, or a People, that have done no right and some good, in and over history?-
    d. Look over our history, and our People, and you will see "it ain't all so black nor white".
    e. Look over our history, and with "Heinz Sight", I am sure we could do all this a thousand times better, and no more.

65. "Silence (now) is as deadly as violence".

And that makes me come back to "Heinz-Sight" again.
Leadership (today) asks us to see what time it is, but to have the vision, heart, courage and can-do to make things better.
    a. To heal, what today is broken.

b. To bear presence and provide a safe holding space for people.
c. To Vision- and re-image the ways things are
d. But not to speak, when times have past, and to know it all (then) better.

66. How do we get the right and capable leadership, with the right mindset, vision, and culture ("being presence") for sustainable societies, in the top of our countries and in our organisations?

    Our present leadership education, talent development, head-hunt- and boardroom election model seems also up for review. Still much too much "old boys school" selection- behavior, thinking and believing - still winning "the Prize". My practice will be most happy to be here with a helping hand- to change!

67. It is very hard for retired senior Leadership to stay in their field of work and change (historic) programmes, worldview, decisions made or belief they defended or created, once they were in

Office. Retired senior leadership in Supervisory Boards or as Advisers to Governments and Officials are hence actually somehow to be suspected: they may stifle true renewal, reform and some creative imaginations and can-do.

68. Wise senior Leadership understands this, and know-how to combine their wisdom and experience, with fresh-minded change-makers.

*"In the beginner's mind there are many possibilities,
but in the expert's there are few."-
Shunryu Suzuki (1905-1971)*

Economy Reform

69. A review of our present and desired market/governance matrix would greatly enhance and benefit results and outcome: a) What can be left to the free market b) Where is government regulation and intervention needed c) Where do both Government and Industry (corporations, market) need to be guided and directed by

an independent expert panel to change (in approach, worldview, realisation) d) where is international/regional diplomacy and influencing required in order to improve good and peaceful outcome- for our Common Home.

70. Now, in this COVID- crisis, this may be the time to start to think the unthinkable once more.- and re-imagine the roles and construct of our (larger than life, too big to fail) businesses in our economies and societies, to re-imagine work, life and income. A review purpose and mission, strategy and organizational frame- into our world post-Covid19: what future and how do we wish them to serve, and how would these organisations look like under plausible and varying circumstances.?

71. Let us direct our work and collective efforts towards attaining:
    a. Well-being economies, that truly serve sustainable development
    b. Energy- Economies - "Free of Concerns"
    c. Societies- "Free of Concerns"

How are we to do this, is our greatest invite. Are we providing words and lip-service to the Great Reset, Building Back Better and our Decade of Action- or are we , and will be for real?

72. We cannot change our Economies, if we do not know how to make room for everybody to be included, and create Societies with governments that People can trust, and where people feel at Peace and at Home.

73. If Nature fails, Economies will falter- and People and Societies will start to become grim- or may start to compete and fight. The People cannot live in Peace if the Planet (Nature) breaks-down, is broken or fails to provide People in their Needs: People will suffer, argue, blame - and may even fight with each other- over the scarcity of resources or the hell they are in.

74. Now the odd reality today is: everything we need is already here.

    We already have all the means, all the technologies, all the wealth and all the know-how to allow and create comfortable, happy and meaningful lives to all.

We can create Blue Skies and local- global connected ecological economies and societies of Unity and Peace.

The simple other reality is: we have created economies, companies and societies that are hold in the interest of the few, not many,

And we have created economies and companies that are unjust in their rivalries and competition - between the have and have nots, the talented and the ones who like to win versus those that still have to learn and are lured to consume , the developed and the developing.

It is in our model of (wealth) distribution and in the caricature of our present (long overdue, neo-liberal and capitalistic) economic system, and our means and believes on market, talent, money, corporation, competition, governance and our position and relationship in and with Nature, that is holding us back .

So- in essence- we have a simple choice to make: 75 years of Hope or Fear. Are you in?

75. Over the past century, we made some great progress and inventions- from Sky Scrapers, Cars, to Airplanes, to Container Cargo Ships, to Plastics, Chemistry and Pesticides, Computers , Social media and the like.

It brought us our present modernities and comfort.

However, we never realized - with the launch of these modern inventions- that the intense use and the (uninhibited) aggregate of these engineered products - would cross a multiple of planetary boundaries (and brings us loss of biodiversity and wildlife, plastic pollution of the Oceans, pollutions and stress in the air- and water ways, loss of original natural forests and land, Climate Change, etc. etc.)- and presently endangers the Natural environment and ourselves.

We were never supposed to drive a 2 billion fuel cars, sit with 4 -to 8 billion passengers in planes, live in mega-cities, are fed by intense, or even, artificial, livestock farming and agriculture, shop in plastified super-markets, - from Indonesia to Brasil, and everything in between.

Our commerce and exploitation of our inventions (in the market place) and our natural world have gone intense, and have become a caricature- of what is normal, or good for us or for Nature.

The aggregate of our present human development is not yet socially just and unsustainable, at best. We consume and have learned ourselves lifestyles and behaviors (and we produce!) , as if there is no tomorrow.

We have made ourselves class(es) of Haves and Have nots, and social justice and equity- in and amongst the Nations- is still an ideal.

76. Our development model is broken and as a human species and in our economic model and markets we run and have become addicted to (rapid) innovation (for what? to what?), a technology slave- and we can be surely concerned about our present hyper- use of Computing, Social Media, - and Artificial Intelligence, Space, Smallest particle(s) and Gen Mod technologies to come.

77. This Covid Crisis, placed in its Context (see above) makes this "unprecedented"- and a crisis complex and of proportion, and making some to nerve and see the possibility of chaos or a break-down, if things turn sour, or another or avalanche of crisis hits our societies in the face:

- Health Crisis
- Finance (debt) crisis
- Economy crisis - market demand, jobs, work and income
- Supply Chains, Globalisation and Trade crisis
- Crisis in Relationships- nationally, internationally.
- Tensions in Geo-Political relationships, Crisis in Global co-operations
- Trust in Future Crisis- new uncertainties

78. We need Humanity back into our Corporations:

Over this year, the Financial Times hosted an on-line Global Boardroom webinar, and conversation series - on the fall-out and learnings from the COVID crisis: Organized at Warp Speed, with the thanks and support by McKinsey Global Institute and E&Y, a wide range and set of "talking heads", were aimed to share realities, clarities, expectations and hope- on this very set and complex deep crisis we see ourselves in.

At times "crystal ball gazing"

Guy Rider of the ILO, Angel Gurria SG of the OECD portrait some pretty dark and gloomy pictures- of a world in present numbers and facts.- and with rapidly unsustainable forms of debt levels rising in corporations and governments.

The rather stoic economists of China radiated extreme confidence on China's abilities to keep a strong economy, and to come well out of this crisis. And to grow.

Many agreed that "the new normal", or the recovery post-COVID-19 will be a different world than we knew before.

The need for a rapid vaccine or cure and "the restoration of trust" are almost unilaterally shared, among the speakers.

Even Tony Blair and Al Gore were taken to stage- to share some words, - and where the latter could not resist to use some angry and hostile words on the present and seating President., and to combine COVID_19 with climate change.
How can we be?

79. What I missed most, if not in all of these (FT Global Boardroom) dialogues and conversations, was a bit of creativity and imagination- as many of the speakers were looking "for solutions" - inside the existing and known playground and playing field. Especially the financial sector and economists are having here the highest words.

Any deeper thoughts on how best to make some new room, balance and direct our economies, and how best to salvage, streamline and much simplify our overburden in financial system,- and to look with new and fresh eyes to the distribution of private and public debts, - 1%- wealthy private and corporate ownership- would have done the conversations some good.

In addition, and these were the consultants, it appeared that all needed to be done "at warp speed", and that recovery is to be gained by more digitization, advanced productivities, smarter supply chains, technology innovation.

Hardly any words were given to "slow down" our economies, to make more room and a better balance for a (local-global) economy where "human values" and "deep ecology values" are better represented and more important than the spreadsheet, competition, efficiencies, productivities or what bankers believed they need to recover from the economy.

80. It was Paul Polman, who almost shyly, dared to pronounce the words: "we need humanity back into our corporations".

81. I have to admit, I have never been a big fan of economists, ministers, bankers or analysts, and who can do remarkable good if not outstanding jobs in "reporting and analyzing what has happened (in the one-dimensional and often their narrow field) " , know where others need to change and are also excellent in presenting and promoting- with good and latest political correct words - their latest achievements, breakthroughs and good works in and to

public and for public attention, and - are making their audiences to believe that they are "in control", and are sure "what is to come, how to change, what needs attention, and how to get this done".

82. More painful even to see, listen and read how Ministers and Institute Heads are selling (own) conventional-, dirty- , hyper- , intense-, digital- ,unproven- , or unnecessary complex or undesirable (energy) technologies, architectures and (policy) solutions (from own country and major energy businesses) to others around the globe.

83. It is and remains important to see with good eyes and listen with good ears- and understand what is said and shared, here- and what not. What remains hidden (unconscious or on purpose) , what is

brewing, what is uncertain, and what is "beyond the veils".

84. What is working and what is not working at all.
    i. Where we are open, collaborative and sharing, and where we are selling, corrupting, competing, or are simply at odds.
    ii. As it is and remains as important to see with own eyes what are the realities in the field, in the varied countries, and on the ground.
    iii. Especially on Energy (Oil & Gas) ("the Prize" - and on and with Security, availability, affordability, sustainability), Paris Climate (, Economy & Money) , and UN SDGs. (and economy ambitions)- and the politics

being played, and the sales and promotions being made.

85. One of a regular joke(s) at my Executive Energy (Transition) workshops and classes has been: "I Wished I could be China for a day"
Now- that is what organisations, can do- and for our very eyes, we may all feel some awe on how this China administration is holding this all together, and what this "grand discipline" in thought and being organised- brings to China and our world.: the positives and pride to its commons, and "the ones who are in", but surely also some grave unease about the negatives, the fears: in people, country, economy and international relationship and Lives.

86. Confucius stated it already in his "Weiyan Dayi"-ways, and where he pointed toward the importance of filial piety which is linked to positive harmonious relationships as well as to the value of hierarchy, order and servant (leadership) excellence.

In his views, hierarchy and positive harmonious relationships do not need to be mutually exclusive or each other's enemy.

Liberal freedom of thought, speech and life, and dignity and respect for (each and every) human life- with(in) order, ritual and serving common grounds, neither.

Organisations, countries and people may be best, when they can handle these two counter-intuitive opposites.

87. Today, many dialogues in the academic and political grounds are on-going on what the difference is between "socially responsible" and "responsible for and/or over societies"- from companies, and in boardroom constellation and R&Rs., and especially when states are weak or failing (in expertise), or the market has become a caricature.

And whether we are to be Kantian or Utilitarian (or Darwinism) in our philosophy over economy, society and our organization forms.- of our governments and larger corporations.

88. Again for people with experience, and eyes to see, - they could ask themselves:

If a working approach (re. Analysis, organisation and policy advice) did not work for the last 20- (50!) years, why would it give us the results we aim for over the coming 10 years?

And

Do we (still) remember that the policies and direction of Climate Action have been lobbied for and formulated by our incumbent (oil and gas) corporations- and were based and chosen on a rather defensive stance from its Leadership (re. to keep oil and gas economy pumping) , and were not to change or transition our energy-economy (architecture) ?

Attempts to reach or set LOFTY goals, is not a PLAN (- for sustainable societies, and our common and shared future).

And in addition,

Our present Leadership (on Energy) misses the point that our agenda over the coming 10 years asks and invites us to see more holistically and work much more on a (multi-dimensional) Energy-Economies-UN SDGs "Free of Concerns".

Without change in our present Economy (Energy-Economy Architecture) , Worldview, Corporate Governance, International Diplomacy, Leadership Style and Approach and our Lifestyles- our very attempts for energy transition are bound to disappoint and fail.

As a Dutch Banker most recently phrased:

The "invisible hand" of Adam Smith needs a heart and brains in our "age of consequences" (climate change, biodiversity loss, pollution, waste, resources scarcity, increasing inequalities, failing health systems): the SDGs are not only offering a comprehensive agenda for society, but also a sustainable and exciting business case; however such perspectives must be enabled and conditioned by "Making Markets fit for SDG Purpose & implementation: a positive system change, with governments to step up in their role as "market-master", and business and society as natural partners "for a better world for everyone".

Lifestyle, Relationships and Habits

89. The term sustainability asks and invites us, like the indegenous people of the world, to live, think, act and work - with compassion and Love- for over 7 generations long: how do my acts, life,

lifestyle today serve those who will come after me (Brundtland definition).

90. We better first solve our present (relationship) problems, make friends with the ones we differ with, before we can make true progress and change.

91. Resistance to change falls when the benefits are made clear. Change is best when we provide People with Hope for their Lives, Families, Homes and Work- better well-being, stronger communities, more trust, better care, more safety, security and comfort

92. Resistance to change falls when the story feels right. Is Human. Touches the Hearts, Souls and Minds. Right Story, Right Frame for the Right Cause and Direction. ("The Star is Chosen Right"). How seldomly is this done well! (People are not robots!)

93. We cannot "run" ourselves into Sustainability. Let us learn to slow down- and walk in more beauty!

94. On the moment we embrace "Deep Ecology and Deep Compassion for Humanity , Nations Traditions and Cultures- and The Ethics of the World Religions" - our world needs and world views changes, the way we "walk, talk and work"., and our wish for "power and control" , "to drive to win", " status" " to show off" in and over our world changes.

95. What grows- is our wish to walk and live life in more beauty. To make Peace and All Good.

96. And how can we expect ordinary people to *see*, *have and enjoy* this more true and better life of Peace and All Good, if our Leaders of their Societies- Political and Corporate- from the East to the West, and the North and the South - "do not get this" , example and amplify something different in their style, story, forms and habits, and do not allow or make the room for healing and this new?

97. Our present approach and orientation to Global Change, Energy-Economy Architecture, Climate and Sustainable Development Agenda does not look fit-

but rather short and shallow- , nor ready to meet important and urgent present, rather real and future planetary and human development targets and goals.

Our present Leadership (in the West) , both political as well in our Corporate Boards and Offices - and who can be responsible, are yet in flock-mantra, are in denial, do not understand or dare to speak about the more complex change challenge we face and are truly in.

"Jolly" is not the right leadership behavior for the program progress mess we have made ourselves in.

We are losing-out in "the old school game" of Oil, Money and Power-politics, and we are losing-out in our ambitions to make the world "Green & Peace".

What we do need is an act of Grace, and whereby we better know-how to integrate and cross the (o so many) Divides, and to come forwards with more healthy ways to **to (true) Peace and Sustainable Development, and making our Energy-Economies Free of Concerns:-**

Change our World View,
Change the way we speak about these issues
Change and reform the Energy economy and the ways the sector operate
Change our economies and market systems
Change the governance, roles and responsibilities of the incumbent energy corporations
Change our lifestyles and consuming habits
Restore our relationships with Nature
Restore our relationships between each other
Restore trust and confidence in our system,

Humanize the way we live, work,
behave, think and act: back to humility
and care.
Become a true messenger of Peace

Gratitude

98. For all the obstacles we see before us, Gratitude and Appreciation should prevail over Concerns and Complaints- Pope Francis.
99. "The world does not want to be saved. The world wants to be loved.
It is through Love (for the World, Nature, People) that we can save our world."- Ana Christina Campos Marques PhD, 2019

Author

Kamp worked 25 years in international project and business development management positions (5 countries) in the Upstream Oil and Gas sector (Shell Group International) and as a private entrepreneur of start-ups. He has grown in his leadership role by progressing a balanced view on our world, society and our individual roles and contributions.

He is committed to servant and conscious leadership and common-wealth. In his role as Founder of Energy For One World, Kamp has formulated a vision and action agenda to progress the (international) energy industry towards a next level of sustainability and leadership over Economy, Society and Nature- blending global needs with local possibility thinking and building bridges between the conventional energy industry with clean-tech.

At Nyenrode Business University, – and also in co-operation with Energy Delta Institute- Kamp has converted this vision into a new-styled Executive Energy (and Energy transition) Training – blending world-class academic thinking on Strategy, Execution and Organizational Change with practitioners and politicians from the energy value chain – advancing strategy and decision making based on this new awareness on the global and local change needs: game-changing the agenda.

Over the years 2014 and 2015, Kamp integrated the above work with the up-and coming UN sustainable development programs, and prepared, defined, authored, presented at Prof Jeffrey Sachs first and early UN SDSN global working conferences at Columbia University. In 2015, Kamp was invited to hold a special college classes at Trinity College in Ireland, and under the guidance of Patrick Walsh (right-hand of Prof Sachs on UN SDSN educational matters)

In year 2016 and in Assisi Italy, and on request of the Franciscans, Kamp formulated a new bridge for the conversion and atonement of Corporate and Government Leadership, and based on Pope Francis Encyclical Laudato Si, the spirit of Assisi and the UN Sustainable Development goals. This work is presently the basis for his program and engagement with the International Franciscan Order in Washington D.C.: Laudato Si in the Boardroom

In 2017- he joined-up with May East, UNITAR fellow and Founder of Gaia Education- and to deepen the collective work "on the edge" of education on the UN SDGs.

Over the year 2018, again, Kamp stepped-up and – amongst others- delivered some consultancy into the energy transition in NW Europe, and was invited to join-in on an "EU-India Bridge Building mission" on Energy, Climate and UN SDGs

For year 2019, Kamp has committed himself to connect some dots and to close some gaps, of where we are today (on Energy, Climate and UN SDGs)- and what may needs done.

Prior to these roles, Kamp started his career as an International Staff member of the Royal/Dutch Shell Group. Following the training in a 9-month international "elite" class to become an "Oilman" in 1986., Kamp subsequently worked and lived in Oman, Norway, Syria and Scotland – in various general management roles in upstream projects – and business development.

Kamp presently consults and speaks on a frequent basis, and on global issues, such as Global Change and our Leadership, UN Sustainable Development, World Energy, Energy Architectures and Transition, Business Strategies and Opportunities, Change and Innovation, CSR/Sustainability and Servant Leadership.

He is also the author of two earlier books: Energy For One World (2012), Tales of Conversion (2017).

Energy For One World

*"**Every Country** and **Every Organization** in this world **can be improved upon** in order to raise the **human, social, economic and sustainable development to all**".*
– Adriaan Kamp, 2016 – Specially Formulated for the UN Sustainable Development Goals

Energy For One World (EFOW) is a boutique consulting firm focused on organizing the delivery of Sustainable Energy Architectures and UN Sustainable Developments into Sustainable Societies. Our hybrid organization is focused on creating and developing outreach programs, consultancy and hands-on programs in, for and between markets and organisations.
With a network of high-level professional relationships crossing the Globe, and with deep expertise in both the Energy Sector and the UN SDG's – from Academia, Business and Government – the EFOW practice is uniquely positioned "to open some new doors", to create

"some new bridges of actions and understanding", to build "cross- border, cross-sector collaborations and impact" and to help to foster "the tone of voice and the leadership values" that are relevant for the changes we may need, or seek.
Since our inception in 2012, we've consistently built and produced new creative forms and formats for Executive Leadership Education, Outreach and Transformative Programs that genuinely are steered to nudge our mainstream corporate and government administrations towards the common goals we seek.

EFOW without Borders (An NGO Foundation Initiative):

We believe in the miracle of human beings. Together we can create a better, healthier and more peaceful world. Our goal by creating this NGO- Foundation initiative is to empower people to learn to lead and act consciously and wisely in order to create a better future.

This initiative is founded on the shared common principles for creating a community of practice. This is based on common values and practical knowledge for building better communities, companies, better lives and a better and healthier planet.

We are faced with serious global challenges, and a welcoming invitation is to make our world a better place to all. As we clearly can see the signs of planetary boundaries, there has been no time in the history of man that the aggregate and wholeness of our human development deserves our wise leadership and attention. Never ever before were we so equipped to build a brighter future to ourselves and all. Never ever were we so reckless and (technological) powerful – that we can and may irreversibly harm our common Home.

We are committed to addressing and acting on these challenges and opportunities by supporting people to become the change makers. We like our leaders to become "Bridge Builders and Peace Makers" and be empowered with the skills, knowledge and practical methods in order to create the road map of working with people, planet and profit- cross cultures, cross borders, cross sectors. Actions and decisions require us to think and act - holistically- and both the short term and long term.

Awareness of where we are today is the first step in making the change to tomorrow and sustainability. We believe that understanding the state of the world today is key in order to make decisions, commitments and most importantly take action in order to build a better future for people, communities and countries which are better balanced for sustaining the health of planet earth. This balance creates happiness and well being for human beginning, which in turn generates income. We cannot have a healthy economy, healthy society, profitable business on a dead or warring planet.

Why we call for this new initiative is because we believe that our time is now in order to create change. Collaboration is the key to bringing people and knowledge when addressing the challenges we face. In order to create a better future, we need to work together, act together and make our movement into programs and positive actions forwards. Creating direct positive impact for people, planet and profit.

EFOW without Borders is to provide a Non-government organisation Foundation initiative that can support outreach, education, consultancy and programs to scale- and be a mirror and counselling help ("coach and care") to those that are presently in Office and Reign- be it in our International Institutions, Government, Corporate Boardrooms and beyond.

www.energyforoneworld.com

www.ingramcontent.com/pod-product-compliance
Lightning Source LLC
Chambersburg PA
CBHW080608220526
45466CB00010B/3286